MAKE A WISH

SCIENTIFIC WAY TO MAKE A WISH SURELY TO BE GRANTED

DR. APASH ROY

Copyright © Dr. Apash Roy
All Rights Reserved.

This book has been self-published with all reasonable efforts taken to make the material error-free by the author. No part of this book shall be used, reproduced in any manner whatsoever without written permission from the author, except in the case of brief quotations embodied in critical articles and reviews.

The Author of this book is solely responsible and liable for its content including but not limited to the views, representations, descriptions, statements, information, opinions and references ['Content']. The Content of this book shall not constitute or be construed or deemed to reflect the opinion or expression of the Publisher or Editor. Neither the Publisher nor Editor endorse or approve the Content of this book or guarantee the reliability, accuracy or completeness of the Content published herein and do not make any representations or warranties of any kind, express or implied, including but not limited to the implied warranties of merchantability, fitness for a particular purpose. The Publisher and Editor shall not be liable whatsoever for any errors, omissions, whether such errors or omissions result from negligence, accident, or any other cause or claims for loss or damages of any kind, including without limitation, indirect or consequential loss or damage arising out of use, inability to use, or about the reliability, accuracy or sufficiency of the information contained in this book.

Made with ♥ on the Notion Press Platform
www.notionpress.com

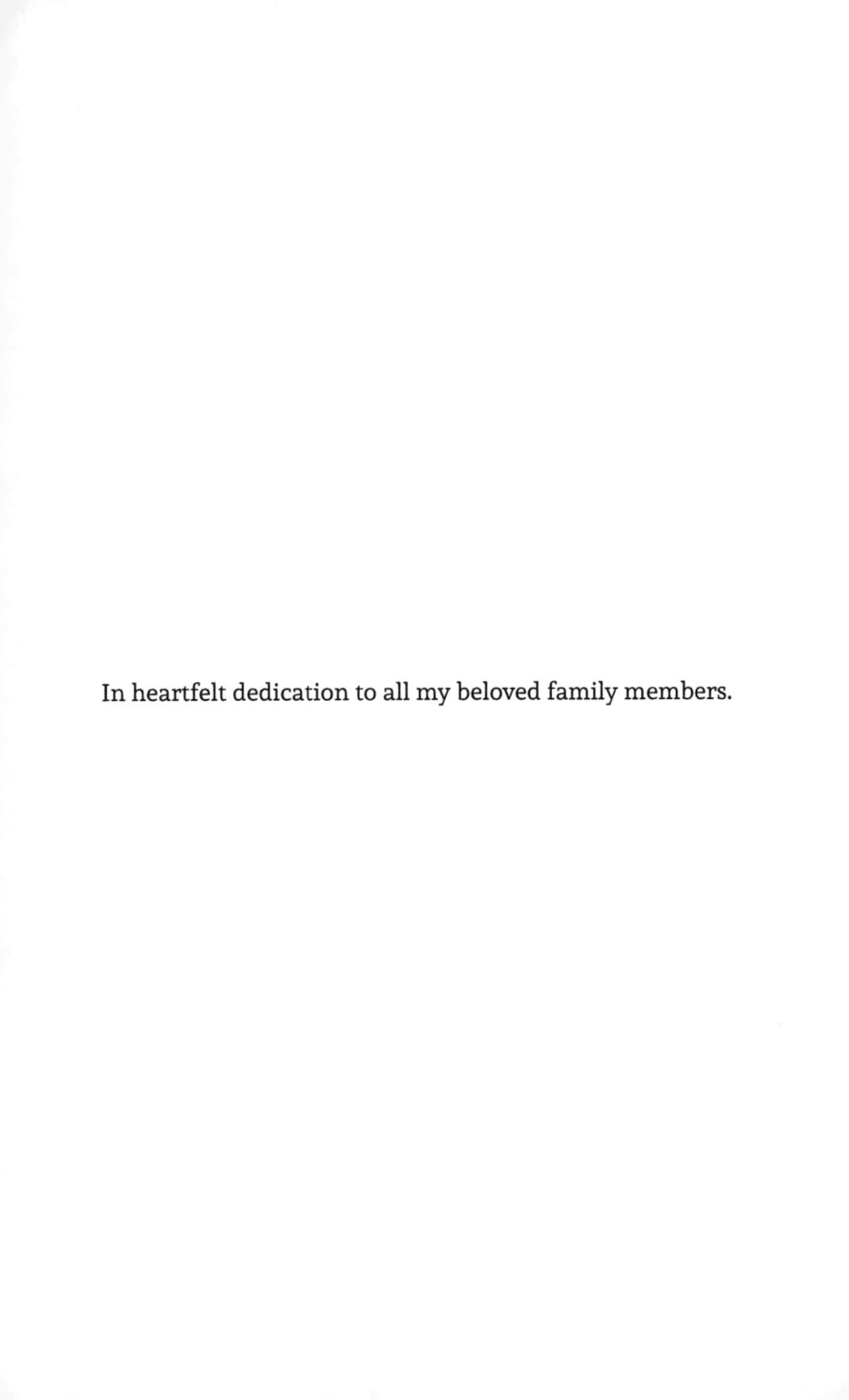

In heartfelt dedication to all my beloved family members.

Contents

Preface   *vii*

1. Wishes In Everyday Life   1
2. What Is A Wish?   10
3. Rise From The Ashes: Story Of Rishav Panth   19
4. The Remarkable Journey Of Joe Dispenza: From Tragedy To Triumph   24
5. The Science Behind Wish   29
6. The Story Of Liza And Her Lucky Penny   36
7. Can Scientific Practice Make A Wish Granted?   43
8. The Rise Of Anaya: A Journey Of Affirmations   50
9. Jim Carrey And The Check Of Destiny: 55
10. Make Your Wish Granted   60

Preface

In a world where desires often clash with reality, the notion of making a wish might seem like a whimsical fantasy. Yet, deep within the realms of science and psychology lies a profound understanding of how our intentions shape our lives. "Make a Wish: The Scientific Way to Make a Wish Surely to be Granted" invites you on a journey that intertwines the power of the human mind with the principles of scientific inquiry, revealing the mechanisms that can transform mere wishes into tangible outcomes.

This book was born from a simple question: What if the act of wishing was not just a fleeting moment of hope, but a powerful catalyst for change? Our exploration begins by delving into the fascinating intersections of neuroscience, psychology, and behavioral science, illuminating how our thoughts, emotions, and beliefs influence our ability to manifest our desires. Through rigorous research and captivating anecdotes, we will uncover the science behind intention-setting, visualization, and the principles of positive psychology.

However, this is not merely a manual for wish-making. It is a guide to understanding the intricacies of the human experience—the hopes we harbor, the fears we confront, and the dreams we chase. Throughout these pages, you will encounter practical exercises and evidence-based techniques designed to harness your innate potential and align your mindset with your aspirations. Whether you seek to improve your personal relationships, advance your career, or cultivate a sense of fulfillment, the tools offered here can serve as your roadmap to success.

As you embark on this transformative journey, I encourage you to keep an open mind and a curious heart. Embrace the idea that the power to change your life lies within you, waiting to be unlocked. The fusion of science and the art of wishing can illuminate your path, helping you navigate the challenges ahead and ultimately guiding you toward a life rich with possibility.

May your wishes take flight and may you discover the incredible potential that resides within you.

—Dr. Apash Roy

1
Wishes in Everyday Life

In the grand tapestry of our daily existence, each thread is woven from our wishes. From the moment we awaken to the moment we close our eyes, our desires influence every action, transforming routine tasks into meaningful experiences.

Wishes in Action

As dawn breaks, the alarm clock signals the start of a new day. Our first wish might be to feel rested and ready to face the day. This simple desire leads to a gentle stretch, a few moments of deep breathing, and a conscious decision to rise. The wish for comfort guides us to adjust the blanket just right before getting out of bed, setting a tone of care for the day ahead.

In the kitchen, the wish for nourishment takes center stage. We may wish for a hearty breakfast to energize us. This desire prompts us to whip up a smoothie or fry an egg, filling the air with comforting aromas. Each bite is a reflection of our wish for health and vitality, transforming a simple meal into a ritual of self-care.

The Journey

Stepping out the door, we might wish for a smooth commute. This desire manifests as we choose our route, perhaps opting for a scenic walk or a podcast-filled bus ride. When we find an empty seat or enjoy a quiet moment, our wish for ease is fulfilled. Each small victory—avoiding traffic or meeting a friend unexpectedly—reinforces the connection between our wishes and our experiences.

Upon arriving at work or school, the wish for connection may arise. We might wish to have engaging conversations or collaborate effectively with our colleagues. This desire inspires us to approach someone we haven't spoken to in a while, leading to a fruitful exchange of ideas. In these interactions, the wishes for camaraderie and inspiration create a vibrant atmosphere, enriching the workplace or classroom.

Moments of Reflection

As noon approaches, another heap of wishes surfaces. We may wish for a moment to relax and recharge. This desire leads us to a favorite café or a peaceful park bench, where we can enjoy our lunch. Savoring each bite becomes a way to fulfill our wish for nourishment and enjoyment, turning a basic meal into a delightful experience.

During lunch, our wishes for connection and laughter often manifest. Sharing a meal with a friend not only satisfies our appetite but also fulfills deeper emotional needs. The conversations that flow over food are rich with camaraderie, highlighting how our wishes for companionship elevate even the simplest of gatherings.

Wind Down

As the day winds down, the wish for productivity comes into play. We might wish to finish household chores or tackle a project. This desire fuels our motivation, leading us to prioritize tasks and create a focused plan. Each completed chore—whether it's doing the laundry or organizing our workspace—becomes a testament to our wish for order and accomplishment.

After a busy day, the wish for relaxation often takes precedence. We might crave a moment of tranquility, prompting us to settle into our favorite chair with a book or a warm cup of tea. This wish for peace transforms our evening into a sanctuary, allowing us to unwind and recharge for the next day.

The Final Moments

As night falls, our final wishes may center around rest and reflection. We may wish to process the day's events, perhaps jotting down thoughts in a journal. This act of reflection allows us to articulate our experiences and intentions, fulfilling a desire for clarity and growth.

Finally, as we close our eyes, our wishes shift to the realm of dreams. We might wish for creativity to flourish or for tomorrow to bring new opportunities. In this space, our aspirations expand beyond the day-to-day, allowing our imagination to take flight. Each dream is an echo of our deepest desires, reminding us that wishes are not just fleeting thoughts but powerful forces shaping our reality.

The Interplay of Wishes and Actions

Throughout the day, it becomes clear that our wishes are not isolated moments; they intertwine and influence each other. Each desire propels us forward, creating a continuous flow that drives our daily activities. By recognizing this interplay, we can approach each task with intention, knowing that our wishes are the heartbeats of our routines.

As we navigate our own days, consider the power of our wishes. Each small act, whether mundane or extraordinary, carries the weight of our desires. Embrace this understanding, and let it guide us in transforming our daily life into a tapestry rich with intention and meaning.

Moments That Define Us

In the intricate fabric of our daily lives, wishes act as unseen threads, weaving together the myriad experiences that shape our existence. Each moment—whether joyous or tumultuous—emanates from a heap of wishes, pulsating with the energy of our desires and dreams. From the tender years of childhood to the tumultuous trials of adulthood, every significant event is underscored by the silent yearning that propels us forward.

The Freedom of Cycling

The first time we grasp the handlebars of a bicycle, it is more than just a mechanical endeavor; it is an embodiment of freedom. The wish to break free from the constraints of childhood echoes in the air as we wobble and teeter, our heart racing with anticipation. As we pedal furiously, the wind caresses our face, a tangible manifestation of our desire for adventure and independence. In that fleeting moment, every uncertain push against the pedals transforms into a dance of triumph, a wish realized in the exhilarating rush of speed and self-discovery.

The First Pimple

Contrasting the exhilaration of cycling is the deep-seated wish for acceptance that accompanies adolescence. The emergence of a first pimple serves as a cruel reminder of the fragility of self-esteem. We wish for clear skin, for the social grace that comes with unblemished youth. This small, seemingly innocuous blemish can feel like a mountain, casting shadows over self-image and confidence. Each glance in the mirror is a negotiation with our self-worth, highlighting how even the most minor physical changes can stir the tumultuous waters of emotion.

The First Fight

Yet, life's journey is not devoid of conflict. The first fight, a cacophony of emotions, arises from the very essence of our wishes for justice and recognition. A disagreement with a friend can shatter the illusion of harmony, igniting a tempest of anger and confusion. In those heated moments, we wish for validation, for our voice to be heard amidst the clamor. The aftermath often leads to reflection—a reconciliation of wishes—where apologies become bridges, reconnecting the hearts that momentarily drifted apart. This experience, while painful, ultimately shapes our understanding of relationships and the complexity of human emotions.

The Weight of Exams

Transitioning from the personal to the academic realm, the wish for achievement manifests vividly during exams. The pressure mounts, a palpable force that envelops we as we prepare for this rite of passage. Each late-night study session is fueled by the wish for success, the aspiration to excel in a world that often equates worth with performance. As we sit before the blank page, anxiety intertwines with hope, creating a potent cocktail of emotions. With every question answered, we weave our wishes into a tapestry of ambition, one that will influence the trajectory of our future.

The School Experience

In the microcosm of school, countless wishes collide and coalesce. We wish for friendship, for the kind of camaraderie that makes even the dullest days vibrant. The laughter shared in hallways and the whispered secrets in classrooms form the bedrock of our social landscape. Yet, beneath the surface, the yearning for acceptance often shadows these connections, reminding us that every relationship is steeped in unspoken desires. The classroom becomes a crucible, forging not just knowledge but also the very essence of who we are.

The Office Odyssey

As we transition into the professional world, a new heap of wishes emerges. In the office, aspirations for recognition and advancement fuel our daily grind. Each project undertaken is not merely a task; it is a manifestation of our wish to carve a niche in the vast expanse of our field. The accolades sought, the promotions dreamed of, each reflects the relentless pursuit of a vision that extends beyond the confines of our desk. Yet, within this realm of ambition, the wish for work-life balance often becomes an elusive goal, a constant negotiation between professional aspirations and personal well-being.

The Passion of Sports

In the arena of sports, the fervent wish for excellence ignites an indomitable spirit. Every practice session is steeped in the desire to improve, to transcend one's limits. The roar of the crowd, the thrill of competition, all resonate with the heartbeats of countless wishes—each athlete yearning for victory, camaraderie, and the joy of the game. The sweat and toil invested on the field transform aspirations into tangible achievements, where triumphs and defeats alike sculpt character and resilience.

The Sweet Pain of a Crush

Amidst the hustle of life, the heart often finds itself entangled in the delicate web of a crush. The wish for love and affection blooms quietly, creating a symphony of emotions that can feel overwhelming. Each stolen glance, each shared laugh carries the weight of unvoiced desires. The exhilaration of hope and the agony of uncertainty dance together, crafting an intricate narrative of longing that colors our everyday life. In this delicate phase, the lines between fantasy and reality blur, reminding us that every wish carries the potential for both joy and heartache.

The First Kiss

As we navigate the labyrinth of burgeoning feelings, the wish for connection and intimacy burgeons within we. The first kiss—a tender convergence of hearts—captures the essence of youthful longing. With every stolen glance and shy smile, we accumulate wishes: for romance, for belonging, and for the exhilarating thrill of being alive in the moment. When lips finally meet, it is as if time suspends itself, each heartbeat echoing the silent wishes that brought we to this delicate juncture. In that electric exchange, the world fades away, leaving only the intoxicating possibility of love.

The Weight of Emotional Breakdowns

Finally, the emotional breakouts we experience reveal the raw vulnerability of our human existence. In moments of despair, when the weight of unfulfilled wishes becomes unbearable, we are reminded of the fragility of our hopes. These breakdowns—though painful—are pivotal moments of catharsis, often leading to profound self-discovery and healing. The wish for clarity and understanding rises from the ashes of turmoil, guiding us toward the light of resilience.

The Tapestry Continues

As we traverse the landscape of our lives, it becomes evident that every experience is intricately interwoven with our wishes. From the exhilarating freedom of cycling to the bittersweet pangs of emotional turmoil, our desires shape the way we engage with the world. Each moment, each heartbeat, reflects the multifaceted nature of our human experience—a rich tapestry of wishes, woven together by the threads of longing, ambition, love, and growth. Embracing this interconnectedness allows us to navigate life with intention, transforming our everyday activities into profound expressions of who we are.

2
What is a Wish?

Wishing is an intrinsic part of the human experience, a universal act that reflects our hopes, desires, and aspirations. Whether we yearn for something small or dream of monumental achievements, wishing acts as a beacon guiding us toward our goals. Here we will explore the concept of wishing, examining its significance in ancient Indian texts, the different types of wishes, their impact and power, techniques for effective wishing, and a structured approach to transforming wishes into reality. We will also delve into historical practices of wishing in ancient India, provide examples of notable incidents, and discuss recent cases in India where wishes have come to fruition.

What is a Wish?

A wish can be defined as a desire for something that is not currently within one's reach. It embodies the longing for improvement, fulfillment, or change in one's life. Wishes can range from simple desires—like wishing for a sunny day—to complex aspirations, such as striving for personal growth or societal change.

The Psychological Aspect of Wishing

Wishing is not merely a passive act; it often sparks an emotional response and activates cognitive processes. When we wish for something, we engage in visualization—creating mental images of our desires. This mental rehearsal can foster motivation and focus, propelling us to take actionable steps toward fulfilling our wishes.

Wishes According to Puranas, Vedas, and Bhagavad Gita

In ancient Indian literature, particularly in the Puranas, Vedas, and Bhagavad Gita, wishes hold significant philosophical and spiritual meanings.

Puranas

The Puranas are ancient texts that narrate the history of the universe from creation to destruction. They often depict wishes in the context of deities and human experiences. For instance, the tale of Vishnu granting boons illustrates how sincere wishes can be fulfilled through divine intervention. The Markandeya Purana tells the story of King Harishchandra, who wished for truth and justice. His unwavering commitment to these ideals led him through trials that ultimately rewarded him with divine blessings.

Vedas

The Vedas, the oldest sacred texts of Hinduism, emphasize the power of Sankalp, or intention. In rituals, practitioners articulate their wishes through sacred chants and offerings, seeking blessings from the gods. The Vedic philosophy teaches that a clearly defined intention can align one's desires with universal forces, making fulfillment more attainable.

Bhagavad Gita

In the Bhagavad Gita, Lord Krishna emphasizes the significance of selfless wishes and desires. He teaches that while it is natural to have desires, they must align with one's dharma (duty) and the welfare of others. The Gita illustrates the concept that wishes rooted in selflessness can lead to spiritual growth and fulfillment.

Types of Wishes

Wishes can be categorized into various types, reflecting the diverse dimensions of human desires.

Personal Wishes

These are individual aspirations related to health, career, relationships, and personal growth. For instance, someone might wish to achieve a promotion at work or develop a new skill. Personal wishes often reflect individual values and priorities.

Altruistic Wishes

Altruistic wishes extend beyond oneself, focusing on the well-being of others and the betterment of society. Examples include wishing for world peace, improved education for underprivileged children, or environmental sustainability. Such wishes underscore our interconnectedness and empathy.

Material Wishes

Material wishes pertain to tangible desires for possessions or experiences, such as wanting a new car, a house, or a vacation. While they may seem superficial, material wishes often signify deeper emotional needs, such as security and fulfillment.

Existential Wishes

Existential wishes delve into the quest for meaning and purpose in life. These may include desires for spiritual growth, enlightenment, or understanding one's role in the universe. Such wishes reflect the human search for identity and significance.

The Impact of Wishes

Wishes profoundly influence our lives and can shape our reality in various ways.

Motivation and Inspiration

Wishes serve as powerful motivators, encouraging individuals to take actionable steps toward their goals. When we articulate our desires, we clarify our intentions, which inspires us to pursue our ambitions. For instance, someone wishing to improve their health may feel motivated to adopt a healthier lifestyle.

Emotional Well-Being

Engaging with our wishes can enhance emotional well-being. Acknowledging our aspirations fosters a sense of purpose and fulfillment. Studies indicate that individuals who practice positive thinking and visualization experience lower stress levels and greater overall happiness.

Decision-Making

Wishes influence our decision-making processes. Clearly defined wishes guide our choices, helping us prioritize what truly matters. For instance, a person wishing to travel may choose to save money or seek employment opportunities that align with their goals.

Social Connection

Wishes can create bonds between individuals. Sharing our wishes with friends and family fosters support and encouragement, building a network that empowers us to pursue our dreams. Collaborative wishing can lead to collective efforts, enhancing community ties.

The Power of Wishes

Wishes possess immense power, shaping our experiences and reality in profound ways.

Positive Thinking and Mindset

Wishing fosters a positive mindset. Focusing on our desires cultivates an outlook that embraces possibilities rather than limitations. This shift in perspective enhances creativity and resilience in overcoming challenges.

Visualization and Manifestation

Visualization is a powerful technique associated with wishing. By vividly imagining our desires, we create mental blueprints that guide our actions. The concept of manifestation posits that focusing on positive thoughts and intentions can attract positive outcomes into our lives.

Spiritual Alignment

In many cultures, wishing is viewed as a form of spiritual alignment. The act of wishing is often accompanied by rituals or prayers that connect individuals to a higher power. This spiritual dimension enhances the potency of wishes, fostering a sense of connection to the universe.

Techniques for Effective Wishing

To harness the power of wishes effectively, individuals can employ various techniques that enhance clarity, focus, and commitment.

Visualization

Visualization involves creating vivid mental images of your wishes. Spend time each day picturing your desires—how achieving them feels, what you will see, and how your life changes. This practice enhances motivation and reinforces your belief in the possibility of success.

Affirmations

Craft positive statements that reinforce your beliefs and intentions. For instance, if you wish for career success, you might say, "I am worthy of success, and I attract opportunities that align with my goals." This practice fosters self-belief and cultivates a mindset open to possibilities.

Gratitude Journaling

Keeping a gratitude journal, where you regularly record things you are thankful for—including progress toward your wishes—can enhance your overall outlook. Expressing gratitude reinforces positive thinking and aligns your mindset with abundance rather than scarcity.

Mindfulness Practices

Incorporate mindfulness into your daily routine to stay connected to your wishes. Take moments to pause, breathe, and reflect on your desires, fostering a deeper awareness of your aspirations.

How Wishing Was Practiced in Ancient India

In ancient India, the practice of wishing was deeply embedded in spiritual and cultural traditions. Wishes were often articulated through rituals, prayers, and mantras, believed to invoke divine blessings and fulfill aspirations.

Examples of Practice in Ancient India

Sankalp: In Hindu rituals, the practice of Sankalp involved setting a clear intention or wish before performing pujas (worship) or yajnas (sacrificial fire ceremonies). Practitioners would articulate their desires, often invoking specific deities to bless their wishes. This process emphasized clarity of intention and spiritual alignment.

Mantras: Sacred sounds or phrases were chanted to invoke specific desires. For example, the Gayatri Mantra is a prayer for wisdom and enlightenment. Reciting mantras was believed to channel divine energy toward fulfilling one's wishes.

Yajnas and Homas: Fire rituals were performed to seek blessings from the gods. Participants would offer various items into the sacred fire while expressing their wishes. The smoke was believed to carry their intentions to the heavens, where deities would grant their desires.

Fasting and Penance: In some traditions, individuals undertook fasting or penance to strengthen their wishes. This practice demonstrated dedication and sincerity, believed to attract divine favor and make their wishes more potent.

A Simple Process of Wishing

Transforming a wish into reality involves a straightforward yet effective process. This journey requires intention, action, and reflection.

Step 1: Identify Your Wish

Begin by clearly defining what you want. Take time to reflect on your desires, exploring what resonates with your heart. Write it down, creating a tangible representation of your wish.

If you wish to start a business, articulate your vision clearly: "I wish to open a successful café in my community."

Step 2: Visualize the Outcome

Imagine yourself achieving that wish. Spend a few moments each day picturing the details—how you will feel, what you will see, and the impact it will have on your life.

Visualize the café filled with customers, the aroma of fresh coffee in the air, and the joy of serving your community.

Step 3: Create an Action Plan

Outline actionable steps you can take to bring your wish to fruition. Break your wish into smaller, manageable tasks. This plan serves as a roadmap, guiding you toward your goal.

Research the café industry, create a business plan, secure funding, find a location, and start the marketing process.

Step 4: Take Action

Consistent action is crucial. Begin working on your plan with determination and focus. Each step, no matter how small, brings you closer to your wish.

Start by researching local regulations for opening a café and securing necessary permits.

Step 5: Reflect and Adjust

Periodically evaluate your progress and reflect on your journey. Celebrate your successes, no matter how minor, and adjust your approach if necessary. Flexibility is key; the path to achievement is rarely linear.

If your initial marketing strategies don't attract customers, consider adjusting your approach based on feedback.

Practicing Wishing in Daily Life

Incorporating the practice of wishing into daily life can be transformative. It requires intention, awareness, and consistency.

Daily Affirmations

Start each day with affirmations that resonate with your wishes. Speak them aloud or write them down to reinforce your belief in your desires.

Visual Reminders

Use visual reminders to keep your wishes in sight. Create a vision board, hang up inspiring quotes, or keep notes in places you frequently visit.

Gratitude Practices

Regularly express gratitude for the progress you make toward your wishes. Acknowledging small victories cultivates positivity and motivation.

Mindful Reflection

Set aside time each week for mindful reflection. Consider your wishes, the progress you've made, and any adjustments you may need to implement.

MAKE A WISH

3
Rise from the Ashes: Story of Rishav Panth

Rishav Panth, the pride of Indian cricket, is known for his explosive batting and charismatic presence on the field. It was a crucial match in the T20 World Cup, and the air was electric with anticipation. Fans filled the stadium, chanting his name. As he strode to the crease, Rishav felt invincible.

But on an intervening night of December 30-31 in 2022, everything changed. A terrible car accident threatened his limb, life and of course his Cricket. He found himself lying face down with his right leg dislocated by 90 degrees. During the treatment in Dehradun and later in Mumbai, India, there was a rare hope of recovery upto a level, where he could walk by himself again.

The Treatment

He received immediate medical attention at a hospital in Dehradun, where he was assessed for various injuries, including head trauma and ligament damage to his knee. Following emergency treatment, Pant underwent surgery to address his injuries. His recovery included a comprehensive rehabilitation program featuring physiotherapy to regain strength and mobility, as well as ongoing medical evaluations to monitor his progress. Psychological support was also integrated into his treatment, acknowledging the emotional impact of the accident

The Determination

Immediately after the accident, he thought the time is over for him in the world. But as he started recovering, he started enjoying even the first time brushing his teeth by himself. He started taking the second life as opportunity and got a strong feeling that he is playing again, thought going to toilet by himself was yet to be achieved. He started trusting the process and visualizing his comeback

After a week of deep reflection, Rishav realized he had two choices: succumb to the darkness or fight back. One night, he lay in bed, staring at the ceiling, feeling the weight of his dreams slip away. Suddenly, an idea struck him. He reached for his phone and typed a message to his coach, a mentor who had always believed in him: "I want to come back."

The next day, with determination in his heart, Rishav set a new goal. He began visualizing himself walking, running, and eventually batting. He created a mantra that echoed in his mind: "I am strong. I will walk again. I will play again."

"Every morning, you need to affirm your strength," his therapist advised. "It's not just about physical recovery; your mind must be in the game too."

The Road to Recovery

Days turned into weeks, and Rishav's world became a battleground. He endured grueling physical therapy sessions, each step feeling like an insurmountable challenge. The pain was excruciating, but he repeated his affirmations like a mantra.

With every inch he gained, his spirit soared. He pushed himself harder, envisioning the moment he would return to the cricket field.

The breakthrough came one sunny afternoon. With gritted teeth and tears of determination, he took his first steps, shaky but resolute. "I can do this!" he shouted, exhilaration surging through him.

The Comeback

Months later, Rishav was back on the cricket field, the smell of grass and the thrill of the game igniting his soul. The sound of leather hitting wood was like music to his ears. He practiced day and night, fueled by a desire that burned brighter than ever.

The selectors were watching, and whispers circulated about his remarkable recovery. "Is he ready?" they questioned. But Rishav had proved his worth through sheer grit. The day the call came for the Indian national team, he felt a wave of elation wash over him.

The World Cup Begins

The World Cup was upon them, and the stakes couldn't be higher. The team had trained hard, but doubts lingered in the shadows. Rishav was determined to silence them.

As the tournament progressed, Rishav played with unmatched aggression, smashing boundaries and scoring runs that sent shivers down the spines of opponents. He was back, and he was unstoppable.

In the semifinals against Pakistan, Rishav faced immense pressure. The team was struggling, and he knew he had to step up. With the weight of a billion dreams on his shoulders, he took a deep breath and let his instincts guide him. The game was thrilling, with every ball creating a pulse of excitement.

In the final overs, he led the charge, hitting sixes that sent the crowd into a frenzy.

The Final Battle

The final match was set against Australia, a fierce competitor known for their aggression. The stadium was packed, and the atmosphere crackled with energy. As the national anthem played, Rishav's heart swelled with pride. He was ready for battle.

With every ball bowled, the tension escalated. Rishav scored quickly, driving the team forward. But disaster struck when he was run out during a tense moment. The stadium fell silent, and for a moment, he felt the world crashing down around him.

But Rishav wouldn't let despair take hold. As he walked back to the pavilion, he whispered to himself, "I am strong. I will fight until the end." He rallied his teammates, encouraging them to dig deep.

The match reached a fever pitch, with India needing 20 runs in the final over. The pressure was immense, but Rishav's determination echoed through the stadium. With every hit, he visualized victory, channeling all the pain and struggle of his journey into those final moments.

Victory and Redemption

With the last ball bowled, India won by a narrow margin. The roar of the crowd was deafening, a symphony of joy and relief. Rishav fell to his knees, tears streaming down his face.

"We did it! We did it!" he shouted, his teammates lifting him in celebration.

As he stood on the podium, holding the World Cup trophy high, Rishav knew this victory was not just about cricket; it was about resilience, determination, and the power of belief.

"I dedicate this win to everyone who believed in me, who fought with me through the darkest times!" he declared, voice ringing out over the cheering crowd.

A Legacy of Hope

Rishav Panth's journey became a symbol of hope and determination. His story inspired millions, proving that with unwavering belief, anything is possible. The road to recovery had been arduous, but in the end, he emerged not just as a champion, but as a beacon of resilience for future generations.

From the ashes of despair, Rishav had risen, and he would forever be remembered as a legend, a warrior, and a hero who conquered the battlefield of life itself.

4
The Remarkable Journey of Joe Dispenza: From Tragedy to Triumph

---

It was a crisp morning in 1986 when Joe Dispenza, a promising young chiropractor with a passion for wellness, set out for a routine bike ride near his home in Washington State. The sun was shining, and the world was filled with the kind of vibrant energy that made him feel alive. As he rode through the peaceful countryside, Joe felt an exhilarating rush of freedom. Little did he know that his life was about to change forever.

In a sudden moment of chaos, a car veered into his lane. Time seemed to freeze as Joe braced for impact, but there was no escaping the collision. The world went dark as he was thrown from his bike, landing with a bone-crushing thud on the asphalt. When he awoke in the hospital, the harsh fluorescent lights illuminated a grim reality: he had suffered multiple fractures in his spine. The doctors delivered the devastating news—he would likely never walk again.

The Diagnosis

Days turned into weeks as Joe lay in his hospital bed, trapped in a body that felt foreign to him. The doctors spoke in hushed tones about surgery, rods, and a long road to recovery filled with uncertainty. Fear seeped into his bones, but alongside it, a flicker of determination began to grow.

In the quiet moments of despair, Joe found solace in the power of the mind. He recalled the teachings of the body's innate healing abilities and how thoughts could influence physical health. This ignited a spark within him, a belief that he could defy the odds. He began to envision his spine healing, visualizing each vertebra aligning perfectly.

The Decision

Against medical advice, Joe made a pivotal choice: he would not undergo the recommended surgery. Instead, he would embark on an uncharted path of healing through the power of meditation, visualization, and sheer will. As he left the hospital, a wave of fear washed over him, but he quickly replaced it with an unwavering determination to heal himself.

Joe established a daily routine centered around meditation. Each morning, he would sit quietly in his living room, closing his eyes and picturing his spine mending itself. He imagined the blood flowing freely, carrying nutrients to every injured cell. The images were vivid and real—his spine radiating light, muscles strengthening, nerves firing with vitality. In those moments of deep concentration, he felt as if he could transcend the physical limitations imposed on him.

The Struggle

But the road to recovery was not without its challenges. There were moments of doubt and despair when the pain threatened to overwhelm him. Friends and family, concerned for his well-being, urged him to reconsider surgery, warning him that his dreams of walking again might lead to disappointment. Yet, Joe remained resolute, drawing strength from the belief that he could heal himself.

As days turned into weeks, he began to feel subtle changes in his body. He could wiggle his toes; it was a small victory, but it fueled his determination. Each improvement, no matter how insignificant, felt like a miracle. He immersed himself in books about the mind-body connection, studying quantum physics and the neuroscience of change, deepening his understanding of the healing process.

The Breakthrough

Months passed, and one day, as Joe engaged in his morning meditation, a profound realization struck him. Healing was not just about visualizing the end result; it was about feeling the emotions associated with that healing. He shifted his focus from the outcome to the process, allowing himself to experience joy, gratitude, and love in every moment.

He began incorporating movement into his practice. With the help of a physical therapist, Joe slowly started to regain strength. Each small step was a victory, and he learned to celebrate the journey rather than the destination. Eventually, after nearly a year of unwavering commitment to his mind and body, Joe stood up. The moment was surreal—he had transformed his vision into reality.

The Triumph

The day he took his first steps was a celebration of the human spirit's resilience. With tears streaming down his face, Joe walked, albeit slowly, with the assistance of a walker. Friends and family gathered around him, stunned by the miraculous transformation. It was a moment of triumph that embodied years of dedication and unwavering belief in the power of the mind.

As he continued to heal, Joe began sharing his story with others, teaching them about the extraordinary connection between mind and body. He became a beacon of hope, inspiring countless individuals to tap into their innate healing potential. His journey of recovery became a testament to the extraordinary power of human resilience, determination, and the mind's ability to shape reality.

A New Path

Today, Dr. Joe Dispenza travels the world, leading workshops and seminars on the mind-body connection, meditation, and healing. He authored several books, including "You Are the Placebo," where he shares the profound insights he gained during his recovery. Joe's story continues to inspire countless individuals to harness the power of their minds to create miraculous changes in their health and lives.

In the face of adversity, Joe Dispenza discovered that true healing lies not just in the physical realm, but in the boundless potential of the human spirit—a reminder that sometimes, the greatest miracles come from within.

MAKE A WISH

5
The Science Behind Wish

The act of wishing—whether it's blowing out birthday candles, tossing a coin into a fountain, or voicing a heartfelt desire—is a universal human experience. It connects us to our dreams and aspirations, often imbued with hope and optimism. But what if there's more to wishing than mere superstition or chance? This chapter explores the intersection of science, psychology, and the principles of manifestation to understand the mechanisms that might explain how wishes can be granted.

1. The Psychology of Wishing

1.1 The Role of Positive Thinking

Psychological research has consistently demonstrated the benefits of positive thinking. Positive affirmations—statements that reinforce one's self-worth and potential—can lead to increased motivation and better outcomes in various areas of life. The power of positive thinking lies in its ability to reshape our mental frameworks, leading to increased resilience and proactive behavior.

Key Studies

- **The Pygmalion Effect:** This phenomenon shows that higher expectations lead to an increase in performance. When we wish for something, it creates a mental image of success, which can enhance our motivation to achieve it.
- **Cognitive Behavioral Therapy (CBT):** CBT emphasizes the importance of reframing negative thoughts. When we wish for something and focus on positive affirmations, we shift our mindset, which can influence our actions and choices.

1.2 The Power of Visualization

Visualization is a technique used in various fields, from sports to therapy, where individuals imagine themselves achieving their goals. Research indicates that visualization activates the same neural pathways as actual experience, which can enhance performance and increase the likelihood of achieving the desired outcome.

Scientific Insight

- **Neuroscience of Visualization:** Brain scans have shown that when we visualize an action, the brain regions involved in executing that action light up as if we are performing it. This suggests that our brain may not distinguish between visualization and reality, which can help in manifesting our wishes.

2. The Law of Attraction

The Law of Attraction posits that positive or negative thoughts bring positive or negative experiences into a person's life. While often considered a spiritual or metaphysical principle, elements of this concept have found their way into scientific discourse.

2.1 Quantum Physics and Consciousness

Some proponents of the Law of Attraction draw parallels with quantum physics, arguing that our consciousness can influence physical reality. While this assertion remains controversial, certain aspects of quantum theory—like entanglement and the observer effect—suggest a complex relationship between consciousness and the material world.

The Observer Effect

- **The Observer Effect in Quantum Mechanics:** This principle states that the act of observation can change the state of a particle. While it's a stretch to claim that wishing can alter reality, it does highlight the complex interaction between perception and existence, hinting at the profound ways our consciousness can shape our experiences.

3. The Science of Goal Setting

Making a wish often aligns closely with goal setting, a process grounded in psychological science. Setting specific, measurable, achievable, relevant, and time-bound (SMART) goals can significantly increase the likelihood of achieving desired outcomes.

3.1 The Impact of Commitment

Research indicates that public commitment to a goal (akin to making a wish) can enhance accountability and motivation. By vocalizing our desires or intentions, we create a social contract that can drive us to take action.

Studies on Commitment

- **Commitment and Self-Determination Theory:** This theory posits that commitment to a goal fosters intrinsic motivation, which can propel individuals towards achieving their wishes.

4. The Role of Action and Effort

Wishing alone isn't sufficient to bring about change; action is a critical component. When we wish for something, we often subconsciously align our behaviors to make that wish a reality. This alignment can be understood through the lens of self-efficacy—the belief in one's ability to succeed.

4.1 Self-Efficacy and Success

Developed by psychologist Albert Bandura, self-efficacy plays a crucial role in how we approach goals. When we believe in our capacity to achieve a wish, we are more likely

to take the necessary steps toward it.
Research Findings

- **Bandura's Studies:** Research shows that individuals with high self-efficacy are more likely to set challenging goals and persist in the face of obstacles, thereby increasing the likelihood of their wishes being granted.

5. *Practical Techniques for Manifestation*

While the science behind wishing and affirmations offers valuable insights, several practical techniques can help turn wishes into reality:

5.1 Affirmations and Journaling

- **Daily Affirmations:** Regularly reciting positive affirmations can help rewire the brain, fostering a mindset conducive to achieving goals.
- **Gratitude Journaling:** Keeping a gratitude journal shifts focus from what is lacking to what is already present, creating a positive feedback loop that can enhance overall well-being and motivation.

5.2 Vision Boards

Creating a vision board is a visual representation of one's goals and wishes. Research indicates that engaging with visual stimuli can enhance motivation and focus.

5.3 Mindfulness and Meditation

Mindfulness practices can help clear mental clutter, allowing individuals to focus on their wishes and aspirations. Studies suggest that mindfulness can enhance emotional regulation and reduce anxiety, making it easier to pursue goals.

Conclusion

While the act of wishing may seem simplistic, the science behind it reveals a complex interplay between psychology, behavior, and consciousness. By understanding the mechanisms that underlie our desires—such as positive thinking, visualization, commitment, and self-efficacy—we can harness the power of our wishes and align our actions to make them a reality. Thus, while the universe may not grant wishes in the fairy-tale sense, our thoughts, beliefs, and actions can create a fertile ground for dreams to flourish, leading us toward a more fulfilling life.

By blending the art of wishing with scientific principles, we unlock the potential to transform our lives in profound and meaningful ways.

DR. APASH ROY

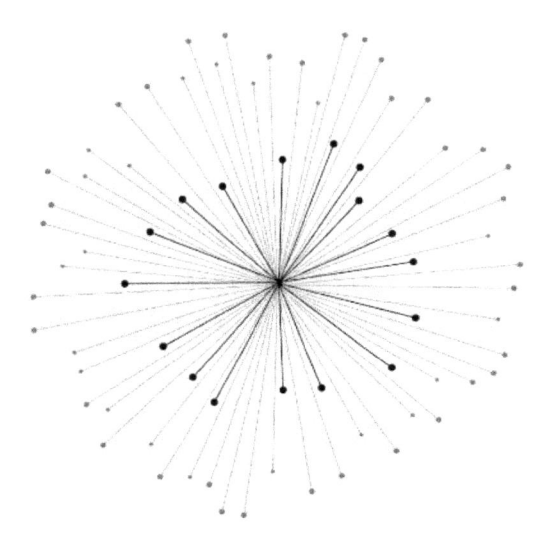

6
The Story of Liza and Her Lucky Penny

Liza Harper was having a rough semester. As a college student juggling part-time jobs and a demanding course load, she felt overwhelmed by her financial burdens. Her student loan debt loomed over her like a dark cloud, threatening to overshadow her dreams of graduating.

One rainy afternoon, she trudged across campus, drenched from head to toe, feeling utterly defeated. As she passed the old oak tree in the quad, something glimmered in the mud. Curious, she bent down to pick it up. It was a penny—dirt-covered but shining in the weak sunlight.

With a sigh, she wiped it off and turned it over in her fingers. "This is ridiculous," she muttered, "but what the hell."

She closed her eyes, made a wish for a way to afford her tuition, and slipped the penny into her pocket. Little did she know that her life was about to take an unexpected turn.

A New Opportunity
The Notification

The following week, Liza received an email that made her heart race. "Congratulations! You have been awarded the Silver Oak Scholarship," it read. The scholarship was worth a substantial sum, enough to cover her tuition for the rest of her college career. She stared at the screen in disbelief.

"How is this possible? I didn't even apply!" she exclaimed, shaking her head.

But the excitement quickly faded as a chill ran down her spine. Why would she, of all people, receive such a windfall?

The Investigation

As Liza reveled in her good fortune, she couldn't shake the feeling that something was off. Who had nominated her for the scholarship? What were the criteria? Determined to find answers, she dug deeper.

That evening, she visited the scholarship office, where she encountered a stern-looking administrator.

"Ms. Harper, the scholarship is quite competitive. You should be aware that some candidates may not be as happy about this decision," the administrator warned cryptically, her gaze unwavering.

Liza felt a knot tighten in her stomach. "What do you mean?"

"You'll need to keep a low profile," the woman replied, her voice laced with urgency. "There are some who don't take kindly to surprises."

The Threat Emerges

Unwanted Attention

The next few days passed in a haze of joy and anxiety. Liza tried to enjoy her classes, but whispers and furtive glances from her peers unsettled her. One evening, while studying late in the library, she noticed a group of students laughing too loudly nearby. When she caught their gaze, their laughter ceased, and their smiles turned into thinly veiled smirks.

"Looks like someone's got a free ride," one of them sneered, flicking his gaze to Liza's desk where she had left her scholarship notification open.

A sense of foreboding crept over her. She felt like a target, and her lucky penny now felt more like a curse.

The Confrontation

That night, as she walked home through the darkened campus, Liza sensed someone following her. Her heart raced, and she picked up her pace. Suddenly, she heard footsteps echoing behind her. She glanced over her shoulder and saw a figure in a hooded sweatshirt, moving quickly.

Panicking, she sprinted toward her dorm, her breaths coming in sharp gasps. The figure gained on her, and just as she reached her building, she stumbled, falling hard onto the pavement.

The Encounter

A hand gripped her shoulder, and she spun around, ready to scream.

"Liza!" a familiar voice said, and she froze. It was Mark, a fellow student she'd spoken to a few times. "I was trying to catch up with you! Are you okay?"

Heart still racing, Liza scrambled to her feet. "I thought someone was following me!"

"Let's get inside," Mark urged, looking around nervously. "This place can be sketchy at night."

As they hurried into the safety of the building, Liza's heart raced, not just from fear, but from the strange connection she felt with Mark. He had a certain intensity about him that both intrigued and frightened her.

The Dark Turn

The Revelation

Over the next few days, Liza and Mark grew closer as they studied together and shared late-night conversations. She confided in him about her scholarship and her fears of being targeted.

"Some people will do anything to sabotage others," Mark warned one night, his expression serious. "Be careful."

Just as she was beginning to feel secure, Liza received a mysterious text message late one night: "We know about the penny. You don't deserve that scholarship. Watch your back."

Chills ran down her spine. Who was sending these messages?

The Ambush

The next day, while walking to class, Liza felt the hairs on the back of her neck stand up. A group of students loomed nearby, and she could see the same faces from the library. They were whispering, casting glances in her direction.

Feeling cornered, Liza hurried toward the student union. But before she could reach it, she was grabbed from behind.

"Hey, scholarship girl! Think you can just waltz in here and take what's ours?" one of the boys snarled, his grip tightening around her arm.

"Let go of me!" Liza yelled, pulling away and stumbling backward. Just as she thought she was trapped, Mark appeared, his face set in determination.

"Get away from her!" he shouted, stepping between her and the aggressors.

The Showdown

Tension crackled in the air as the two groups faced off. Liza's heart raced as she realized Mark wasn't just a fellow student—he was her protector.

"Liza deserves that scholarship more than any of you!" Mark declared, his voice steady. "You're just jealous!"

The aggressors exchanged glances, their bravado faltering. "This isn't over," one of them spat before they retreated into the shadows.

The Resolution
The Unraveling

After the encounter, Liza and Mark spent more time together, growing closer as they shared stories and fears. He helped her file a report about the harassment, and she felt empowered by his support.

One night, while sitting on a bench overlooking the campus, Liza pulled out her lucky penny. "I can't believe this little thing turned my life upside down," she mused.

"Maybe it's a reminder that even small things can have a big impact," Mark replied, a smile lighting up his face.

Suddenly, Liza noticed a shadowy figure watching them from a distance. "Mark, do you see that?"

But when Mark turned, the figure was gone. "Let's head back inside," he said, a note of urgency in his voice.

The Confrontation

Later that week, Liza received another anonymous message: "You won't keep the scholarship. We'll make sure of it."

Feeling a mixture of fear and resolve, she decided to confront the situation head-on. She contacted the scholarship committee to report the harassment and enlisted Mark's help to gather evidence.

One evening, as they waited for the committee's decision, Liza heard a knock at her dorm door. Opening it, she was met with a chilling sight: a group of students from the previous encounters stood before her, anger boiling in their eyes.

"This isn't over, Liza!" one of them hissed. "You'll regret taking what's rightfully ours!"

The Climax

The Showdown

Feeling cornered and frightened, Liza took a deep breath, clutching her lucky penny in her palm. "You don't scare me," she said, her voice trembling but steady.

"Watch your back," one of the students growled before they retreated down the hall, leaving Liza and Mark shaken but resolute.

The Turning Point

A few days later, Liza received a call from the scholarship committee. "We've investigated your claims and found substantial evidence of harassment. We are here to support you," the committee chairwoman said.

Tears of relief filled Liza's eyes. "Thank you," she whispered, feeling the weight lift off her shoulders.

Mark squeezed her hand, a proud smile spreading across his face. "You did it, Liza. You stood up for yourself."

A New Beginning

Months passed, and the harassment ceased after the committee took swift action. Liza continued to thrive academically and socially, her confidence bolstered by her experiences.

One sunny afternoon, she and Mark stood beneath the old oak tree where she had found the penny.

"I think it's time to let this go," she said, holding up the penny.

With a smile, she tossed it into the nearby fountain. As the water splashed around it, Liza felt a surge of freedom. "I'm ready for whatever comes next."

With Mark by her side, she knew that challenges would come, but she was prepared to face them head-on. With a heart full of hope and a spirit unyielded, Liza stepped forward into her future, ready to embrace all the possibilities life had to offer.

7
Can Scientific Practice Make a Wish Granted?

The act of wishing is an intrinsic part of the human experience, imbued with hope, longing, and the desire for transformation. While wishing often feels like an exercise in fantasy or superstition, emerging research in psychology and behavioral science suggests that there may be concrete, scientific processes that can align our intentions with reality. This chapter explores the intersection of scientific practices, psychological insights, and personal agency to reveal how wishes can transition from mere thoughts to tangible outcomes.

1. Understanding Wishes

The Nature of a Wish

At its core, a wish is a desire for something that may currently feel out of reach. Whether it's a personal goal, a dream, or an aspiration, wishes can serve as powerful motivators. They inspire us to take action, set goals, and envision a future that resonates with our deepest values. However, for a wish to become reality, it must be transformed from a fleeting thought into a structured intention.

The Role of Intention

Intention is a critical element in the process of making a wish come true. It involves committing to the desire and aligning one's thoughts and actions toward its fulfillment. Research shows that intentions serve as a bridge between wishful thinking and actionable steps, laying the groundwork for eventual success.

2. The Scientific Approach to Making Wishes Come True

Scientific practice encompasses various methodologies that rely on empirical evidence and systematic observation. By applying scientific principles to the process of wishing, individuals can create a structured pathway that enhances their likelihood of achieving their desires.

Setting Clear Goals

The first step in the scientific approach is to translate a wish into a clear and actionable goal. This is often referred to as the SMART criteria:

- **Specific**: Define exactly what you want to achieve.
- **Measurable**: Establish criteria to track progress and success.

- **Achievable**: Ensure that the goal is realistic and attainable.
- **Relevant**: Align the goal with personal values and long-term objectives.
- **Time-Bound**: Set a deadline to create a sense of urgency.

Suppose your wish is to improve your health. Instead of wishing to "get healthier," a SMART goal would be: "I will exercise for at least 30 minutes, five days a week, for the next three months."

Developing a Plan of Action

Once a goal is set, the next step is to outline a specific plan of action. This involves breaking the goal down into smaller, manageable steps, each with its own timeline and measurable outcomes.

Steps to Create an Action Plan:

1. **Identify Resources**: Determine what tools, skills, or support you need to achieve your goal.
2. **Create Milestones**: Establish smaller milestones that lead to your larger goal. Celebrate these achievements to maintain motivation.
3. **Set a Schedule**: Allocate time in your daily or weekly routine to focus on working toward your goal.

Harnessing the Power of Visualization

Visualization is a scientifically validated technique that involves imagining the successful attainment of your wish. This practice can stimulate the brain and activate neural pathways associated with goal achievement.

Studies in neuroscience suggest that visualization can enhance performance by activating the same brain regions involved in actual execution. This creates a mental rehearsal effect that prepares individuals for real-world challenges.

One may try Spending a few minutes each day visualizing yourself achieving your wish. Engage all your senses—see, hear, and feel the experience as if it were happening in real time.

Cultivating a Positive Mindset

The belief that you can achieve your wish is crucial. Positive thinking and self-efficacy—the belief in one's ability to succeed—play significant roles in motivation and perseverance.

Techniques to Foster a Positive Mindset:

1. **Affirmations**: Use positive affirmations to reinforce your belief in your ability to achieve your goal.
2. **Gratitude Journaling**: Maintain a gratitude journal to focus on positive aspects of your life, which can improve overall well-being and motivation.

Tracking Progress and Adjusting the Plan

A scientific approach emphasizes the importance of monitoring progress and being flexible in your strategies. Regularly evaluate your progress against your milestones and make adjustments as needed.

Strategies for Tracking Progress:

- **Keep a Journal**: Document your journey, noting successes, challenges, and insights.
- **Use Technology**: Employ apps or tools to track your habits and milestones.

Building a Support Network

Social support is critical in the process of making wishes come true. Surrounding yourself with positive influences and accountability can enhance your motivation and resilience.
Ways to Build a Support Network:

- **Find a Mentor**: Seek out individuals who have achieved similar goals for guidance and inspiration.
- **Join a Community**: Engage with groups or online forums that share your interests or aspirations.

3. Overcoming Challenges and Staying Resilient

Even with a scientific approach, obstacles will inevitably arise. Building resilience is crucial for maintaining momentum when faced with setbacks.

Embracing Failure as a Learning Opportunity

Instead of viewing failure as a definitive end, approach it as a learning experience. Analyze what went wrong and adjust your plan accordingly.

Practicing Mindfulness

Mindfulness practices, such as meditation, can help manage stress and maintain focus. Regular mindfulness exercises can cultivate a sense of awareness that enhances emotional regulation and decision-making.

4. The Role of Reflection and Gratitude

As you progress toward your goal, taking time to reflect on your journey is essential. Reflect on the lessons learned, the progress made, and the qualities developed along the way.

Celebrate Achievements

Regardless of size, celebrate your achievements. Acknowledging your successes reinforces positive behavior and keeps you motivated.

Cultivate Gratitude

Practicing gratitude not only fosters a positive mindset but also reinforces the behaviors that lead to success. Regularly expressing gratitude can deepen your commitment to your goals and enhance your overall well-being.

A Synergistic Approach to Wishing

The scientific practice of making a wish granted involves a systematic approach that includes goal setting, planning, visualization, mindset cultivation, progress tracking, and building a supportive network. While the act of wishing may seem whimsical, applying scientific principles to the process creates a tangible pathway for transforming aspirations into reality.

By actively engaging in this process and committing to personal growth, individuals can harness the power of their wishes, turning dreams into achievable goals, and ultimately, reality. The journey of making a wish granted becomes a testament to the synergy between hope, action, and the scientific method—illustrating that, indeed, wishes can be granted when approached with intention and determination.

8

The Rise of Anaya: A Journey of Affirmations

The rain lashed against the windows of St. Mary's High School in Mumbai, a rhythmic drumming that seemed to echo Aanya's racing heart. It was the night before the final exams, and the pressure hung thick in the air like the humidity of the monsoon. Aanya, a bright but anxious student, stared at her books, but the words blurred as her mind spiraled into a whirlwind of doubt.

"Why can't I be like everyone else?" she thought, her thoughts as heavy as the rain outside. With each tick of the clock, her anxiety grew. Every failure echoed in her mind, reminding her of past mistakes. She wished for confidence, for the ability to tackle the exams with ease.

As she fought back tears, her mother entered the room, her expression a mix of concern and love. "Aanya, how about we try something different this time? I heard about a new program at school focusing on affirmations and visualization. It might help you."

Aanya was skeptical. "Mom, how can saying positive things change anything? I can barely remember the formulas!"

But her mother's insistence piqued her curiosity. Perhaps it was worth a shot.

The Introduction of a New Way

The next day, the classroom buzzed with excitement. Mrs. Iyer, their enthusiastic new teacher, stood before them with a sparkle in her eye. "Welcome to the Affirmation and Visualization Workshop!" she announced. "Today, we will explore the power of positive thinking and how it can change your lives—especially when it comes to exams."

Aanya sat in the back, arms crossed, doubtful. But as Mrs. Iyer shared stories of students who transformed their academic lives using these techniques, Aanya found herself intrigued. The energy in the room shifted.

Mrs. Iyer guided them through their first visualization exercise. "Close your eyes and imagine yourself walking into the exam room, feeling calm and confident. Picture yourself answering questions with ease. Feel the joy of success."

Aanya closed her eyes, her skepticism melting away. For the first time, she saw herself at the front of the class, answering questions effortlessly.

"Now," Mrs. Iyer said, "let's create affirmations. Repeat after me: 'I am capable. I am prepared. I will succeed.'"

As the class echoed the words, Aanya felt a flicker of hope ignite within her.

The First Test

Weeks passed, and the exam approached. Aanya diligently practiced her affirmations each morning, reciting them in front of her mirror. "I am capable. I am prepared. I will succeed." She visualized herself taking the exam, the room filled with light and confidence.

But the night before the exam, doubt crept back in. Aanya lay awake, listening to the rain pouring outside. The storm outside mirrored the one inside her head. "What if I fail? What if I forget everything?"

Suddenly, her phone buzzed with a message from her best friend, Meera: "You got this! Just remember our affirmations!"

That small reminder snapped Aanya back to the moment. She sat up, took a deep breath, and repeated her affirmations, feeling the words anchor her.

The Exam Day

The morning of the exam dawned cloudy, the rain subsiding but leaving a cool mist in the air. Aanya walked into the exam hall with Meera, her heart racing. As they settled into their seats, Aanya took a deep breath and closed her eyes. "I am capable. I am prepared. I will succeed."

The exam paper was distributed, and as Aanya opened it, a wave of panic hit her. The questions felt like a labyrinth, twisting and turning in her mind. For a moment, she faltered, her old fears surfacing.

Then she remembered her practice. She took a deep breath, visualized her success, and let the words of her affirmations wash over her. Slowly, the storm inside her calmed, and she began to write.

The Revelation

Days later, the results were posted on the school notice board. A crowd gathered, buzzing with anticipation. Aanya pushed through, her heart pounding. She scanned the list, anxiety clawing at her.

Then she saw it. Her name, right at the top—*Top Scorer in Class 10.*

A wave of disbelief washed over her. She stood frozen, staring at the paper. "Is this real?"

Meera squealed, pulling Aanya into a tight hug. "You did it! I knew you could!"

Aanya's heart raced, a mix of disbelief and joy. She had done it. The affirmations, the visualizations—they had worked.

The Celebration

That evening, Aanya sat on her bed, the results still fresh in her mind. The rain had returned, a gentle patter against the window. She took out her journal and wrote: *I am capable. I am prepared. I will succeed.*

Her mother knocked and entered, beaming with pride. "I'm so proud of you, Aanya! You've proven that the mind can change our reality."

Aanya smiled, her heart swelling with gratitude. She had battled her fears and emerged victorious, a testament to the power of positive thinking.

The Impact of Change

The success of the affirmation program spread throughout St. Mary's High School. Students who once struggled with anxiety found their voices and confidence through the power of affirmations and visualization.

As for Aanya, she became a mentor for others, sharing her journey and teaching her peers the magic of positive thinking. In the heart of Mumbai, amidst the hustle and bustle, a quiet revolution of thought had begun—proving that sometimes, the greatest battles are won not with might, but with belief.

MAKE A WISH

9
Jim Carrey and the Check of Destiny:

The neon lights of Hollywood flickered like stars in the dark sky, casting a glow over Jim Carrey as he stepped out of his beat-up car. A feeling of excitement mingled with despair churned in his gut. The streets were alive with ambition and dreams, but all he felt was the weight of failure.

He had been in Los Angeles for years, grinding through countless auditions, but the big break he longed for seemed as elusive as the stars above. His laughter was a facade, masking a profound fear that he would never make it as an actor.

One evening, after a particularly brutal rejection, Jim sat alone in his small apartment. Desperate for a change, he remembered something his father had told him about the power of intention. On a whim, he picked up a pen and a blank check from his desk. With a surge of determination, he wrote, "Pay to the order of Jim Carrey: $10,000,000. For acting services rendered." He signed it and dated it for Thanksgiving 1995.

The Talisman

Jim slipped the check into his wallet, the thin paper feeling like a talisman against his mounting doubts. Every day, he would take it out, study it, and visualize himself as a successful actor—walking the red carpet, winning awards, and, most importantly, receiving that $10 million paycheck.

The visualization was a daily ritual. In the mirror, he would practice his acceptance speech, picturing the applause, the lights, and the camera flashes. "I am a successful actor," he would affirm. But as the days turned into months, the weight of reality pressed down harder.

The Breakthrough

It was the fall of 1994 when Jim received a call that would change everything. He had auditioned for a quirky comedy film called *Dumb and Dumber*. The casting director wanted to see him again, and this time, he was told to bring his best friend for the audition.

"Bring your best friend?" Jim muttered, a mix of anxiety and excitement bubbling in his chest. His friend, a fellow comedian, joined him for the read. The chemistry between them was electric, and for the first time, Jim felt alive in front of the camera.

Weeks passed, filled with rehearsals and anticipation. But as the filming approached, doubts crept back in. Could he really pull this off?

The Unexpected Twist

As the day of filming loomed closer, Jim faced a critical moment. During a late-night rehearsal, he tripped over a cable and fell hard on the stage, twisting his ankle. Pain shot through him like fire, and he lay there, gasping.

The director rushed over, concern etched on his face. "Are you okay, Jim?"

"I'll be fine!" Jim grunted, his spirit refusing to break. But in that moment, the fear of losing his shot surged back.

He closed his eyes and thought of the check in his wallet, a reminder of his dream. "I am a successful actor," he whispered, letting the affirmation wash over him like a healing balm. The next morning, he woke up to find the pain diminished.

The Day of Reckoning

The set of *Dumb and Dumber* was electric. Jim stepped onto the set, a surge of adrenaline pushing him forward. As he donned his costume, he felt a mix of nerves and excitement. Today was the day he would prove to the world that he was destined for greatness.

As filming began, Jim tapped into every ounce of his creativity, bringing his character to life with hilarious antics and heartfelt moments. The laughter of the crew echoed around him, fueling his performance. He lost himself in the character, each take better than the last.

Finally, the moment arrived. As he wrapped up his scenes, the director approached him, a broad grin on his face. "Jim, this is brilliant! We've got something special here."

The Miracle Unfolds

Months later, Jim received a call that set his heart racing. The film was a hit, and he had been offered a paycheck—$10 million. The words echoed in his mind, each syllable bursting with disbelief.

He rushed home, adrenaline coursing through his veins. He pulled out his wallet, trembling, and unfolded the crumpled check he had written years ago. "Pay to the order of Jim Carrey: $10,000,000." He couldn't believe it.

The date on the check had passed, but the miracle had arrived nonetheless.

The Acceptance Speech

On the night of the Academy Awards, Jim stood backstage, heart pounding, his palms sweaty. He had visualized this moment for years, and now it was here. As he waited for his category to be announced, he glanced at the check in his pocket.

When they called his name, he felt a rush of disbelief and joy. The audience erupted in applause as he walked to the stage, each step solidifying his belief in himself.

"Thank you! I wrote myself a check for this moment," he began, his voice steady, filled with gratitude. "It may sound crazy, but I visualized this day, and I believed in it so strongly that it became my reality. If you believe in your dreams, if you affirm your worth, anything is possible!"

The crowd cheered, and in that moment, he realized that the journey was not just about the money; it was about faith, perseverance, and the power of the mind.

The Legacy of Belief

Years later, Jim would share his story on stages around the world, inspiring countless individuals to believe in their dreams and harness the power of visualization and affirmations. The check was no longer just a piece of paper; it was a symbol of hope, resilience, and the magic of believing in oneself.

As he often said, "You can do anything you want in life if you just believe." And with that belief, he turned the impossible into the possible, proving that dreams, no matter how far-fetched, can become reality with a little faith and a lot of determination.

DR. APASH ROY

10
Make your Wish Granted

Wishing is a universal act that signifies our hopes, desires, and aspirations. It is more than just a fleeting thought; it can be a powerful catalyst for change when approached with intention and mindfulness. Here, we will explore the ideal practices for making wishes that can manifest into reality and how to incorporate these practices into our daily lives. By doing so, we can align our intentions with our actions and foster a sense of empowerment as we navigate the journey toward our desires.

Understanding the Nature of a Wish

Before diving into the practices of making wishes, it's essential to understand what a wish truly represents. A wish is a manifestation of desire, a statement of intention that reflects what we yearn for in life. It can be personal, professional, or spiritual, encompassing anything from health and happiness to success and fulfillment.

The Psychology of Wishing

Wishing engages our imagination and emotions. When we articulate our desires, we create mental images that motivate us to pursue those aspirations. Psychologically, wishing can serve as a form of goal-setting, helping us clarify what we want and fostering a mindset geared toward achieving those desires.

The Ideal Practice of Making a Wish

Creating a wish that can be granted ideally requires a mindful and structured approach. Here are several steps to practice:

Step 1: Define Your Wish Clearly

- **Be Specific**: Rather than wishing for "happiness," define what happiness looks like for you. For example, "I wish for a fulfilling job that allows me to express my creativity."
- **Write It Down**: Documenting your wish reinforces its importance. Consider creating a "wish journal" where you can write and revisit your desires.

Step 2: Connect Emotionally

- **Feel the Wish**: Connect emotionally with your wish. How will you feel when it is granted? Engaging your emotions creates a deeper connection and amplifies

your motivation.
- **Visualize the Outcome**: Spend time visualizing your wish coming true. Imagine the sights, sounds, and feelings associated with achieving that desire. Visualization can enhance motivation and clarity.

Step 3: Set Intentions

- **Positive Intentions**: Frame your wish positively. Instead of wishing to avoid failure, focus on the success you want to achieve.
- **Align with Values**: Ensure your wish aligns with your core values and beliefs. A wish that resonates with your values is more likely to manifest.

Step 4: Create an Action Plan

- **Break It Down**: Divide your wish into smaller, actionable steps. This makes the process more manageable and less overwhelming.
- **Set Realistic Goals**: Ensure your goals are achievable within a reasonable timeframe. This encourages a sense of accomplishment and progress.

Step 5: Take Action

- **Start Small**: Begin with small, manageable actions. Consistent steps can create momentum toward your larger wish.
- **Stay Committed**: Dedicate time each day or week to work on your action plan. Commitment is key to turning wishes into reality.

Step 6: Reflect and Adjust

- **Evaluate Progress**: Regularly assess your progress toward your wish. Are you moving closer, or do you need to adjust your approach?
- **Be Flexible**: If you encounter obstacles, be open to adjusting your plan. Flexibility allows you to adapt to changing circumstances and maintain your focus on the end goal.

Integrating Wishing Practices into Daily Life

Incorporating wishing practices into your daily routine can transform your mindset and enhance your journey toward fulfillment. Here are some strategies to make wishing a regular part of your life:

1. Daily Affirmations

Start each day with positive affirmations related to your wishes. For instance, if you wish for a successful career, affirm: "I am capable of achieving my professional goals."

2. Vision Boards

Create a vision board that visually represents your wishes. Include images, quotes, and symbols that resonate with your aspirations. Place it somewhere you see daily to reinforce your desires.

3. Gratitude Journaling

Maintain a gratitude journal to acknowledge the progress you make. Writing down what you're thankful for fosters a positive mindset and reminds you of your accomplishments, no matter how small.

4. Mindfulness Meditation

Incorporate mindfulness meditation into your routine to stay present and focused on your wishes. Spend a few minutes each day in quiet reflection, visualizing your desires and cultivating a sense of calm.

5. Surround Yourself with Positivity

Engage with uplifting content—books, podcasts, and inspiring people who support your wishes. A positive environment fosters motivation and reinforces your aspirations.

The Role of Community in Wishing

Sharing your wishes with supportive friends, family, or community can amplify their power. Here are a few ways to leverage community support:

1. Accountability Partners

Find someone who shares similar aspirations or desires. Together, hold each other accountable for taking steps toward your wishes.

2. Group Discussions

Participate in group discussions or workshops focused on personal development and goal-setting. Engaging with others can provide new perspectives and encouragement.

3. Celebrate Successes Together

Celebrate milestones, both big and small, with your community. Recognizing achievements can create a sense of collective joy and motivation.

Make a wish

Making a wish is a beautiful and powerful act that, when practiced intentionally, can lead to transformative experiences. By understanding the nature of wishes, following structured practices, and integrating these practices into daily life, we can create a path toward achieving our desires. Embrace the journey, cultivate your wishes, and take proactive steps toward manifesting them. Remember, every wish is an opportunity waiting to be realized—so make a wish, and take the first step toward turning it into reality.

MAKE A WISH

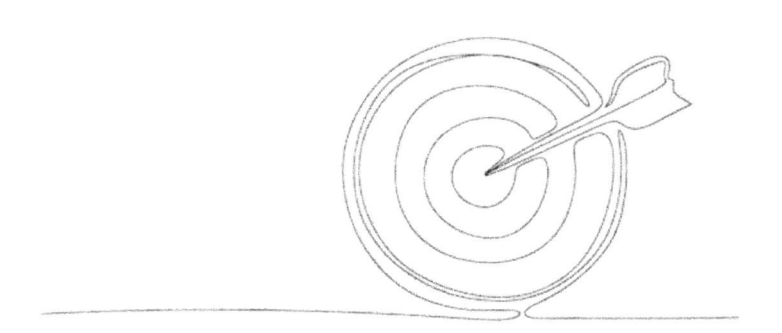

Milton Keynes UK
Ingram Content Group UK Ltd.
UKHW030639191124
451300UK00006B/88